TRANSFORM YOUR LIFE

TRANSFORM YOUR LIFE

SUSURROS DE CHAMÁN

TRANSLATED BY
ESTRELLA HURTADO

I dedicate this book...

To those people in whom I dwell in your heart.

INDEX

Foreword

My name is Estrella Hurtado, and I am the official translator of "Transforming Your Life." I am originally from Chihuahua, Mexico, and I am currently residing in Vancouver, Canada.

I would like to thank the Shaman, who has been my guide for the past few years during my awakening when I needed it the most. My life has been positively transformed since then, thanks to his enlightened wisdom and love.

I am incredibly grateful to have met the Shaman, who has become my spiritual mentor. I hope that he can provide the same guidance and support to anyone who accepts it.

This serves as a reminder to anyone who feels lost in the darkness that there is always a light at the end of the tunnel. Just reach out your hand, and we will be there to hold it.

Personally, it took me years and numerous sessions to fully understand every word written in this book. Therefore, I am delighted that it is now accessible to everyone. "Transforming Your Life" is a remarkable book that surpasses expectations and offers various perspectives on life.

If you are starting your spiritual journey, do not give up, you are not alone. I bless you and wish for you to enjoy every process and embrace your emotions. Also, if you have already begun, I congratulate you on your progress. Just as you have come a long way, you will understand that this book can guide future generations.

I invite you to share your light, your magic, and this book.

PRESENTATION

Transform your life is a book that seeks to guide you on your path of personal and spiritual growth. In its pages you will find tools and practical advice to face your fears, overcome your limits and achieve your goals. From the importance of self-esteem and emotional regulation, to the law of attraction and gratitude, this book will provide you with a variety of tools to help you find the happiness and fulfillment you deserve.

You will learn how the language you use affects your thoughts, emotions and how you can change it to improve your mental and emotional well-being.

You will also explore the importance of spiritual connection and how it will help you find your purpose and meaning in life.

This book will also teach you how to handle uncertainty, change, and how you can turn your mistakes and failures into opportunities for growth and learning.

You'll discover how to practice mindfulness to reduce stress and anxiety, and how gratitude can improve your outlook and life in general.

Transform Your Life is a useful guide for anyone looking to improve their emotional well-being, find their purpose, and create a fuller, more fulfilling life.

Through its practical and accessible approach, this personal book will help you with the necessary tools to face your challenges and achieve your spiritual goals.

Introduction

The author of this book, known as the Shaman, has helped many people transform their lives through his publications and consultancies.

The Shaman believes that we all have the potential to transform and reach our true nature, but we often get lost in the chaos of daily life, routines and stray from our true path.

In this book, the Shaman will guide you so that you learn to free yourself from the limitations that prevent you from growing and show you how to transform your life so that you can reach your full potential.

To help you on this path, the Shaman provides you with three fundamental tools:

The first is the practice of mindfulness, so that you can be present in the moment and free yourself from the stress that prevents you from moving forward.

The second tool is the law of attraction, which will teach you how to attract what you want into your life and manifest your dreams and goals.

And the third tool is the power of action, so you can move from theory to practice and really transform your life.

With these tools, the Shaman will take you on a transformative journey of self-discovery and personal growth, helping you find your purpose and free yourself from the limitations that have been holding you back.

This book is for anyone who wants to reach their full potential and significantly transform their life.

Why is it important to transform our lives?

Spiritual awakening is a transformative experience that can lead to profound changes in our lives. It is a process that allows us to explore our true nature and find a deeper sense of purpose and meaning in life. Spiritual transformation is not a one-off event, but rather an ongoing journey of self-discovery and personal growth.

We have all experienced moments in life where we wonder if there is more to life than what we are currently experiencing. It can be a feeling that something is missing in our lives, or just a general restlessness that there is something beyond what we can see and feel. This feeling is the spark that ignites the spiritual search.

The spiritual search is a search for the truth. It is the search to understand our own existence and the purpose of our life. The spiritual search is an internal search, an exploration of our own being.

It is a journey that takes us beyond the limitations of our mind and allows us to experience our true nature. Spiritual transformation allows us to look beyond the limitations of our mind and find a deeper connection to our inner being.

As we open up to the truth of our existence, we begin to experience a sense of inner peace and greater mental clarity.

This is the path to enlightenment.

Enlightenment is a state of consciousness that allows us to experience life in its fullness.

It is a transformative experience that takes us beyond the limitations of our mind and allows us to experience the true nature of life.

When we are enlightened, we experience a sense of inner peace and a deeper connection to the universe.

Spiritual transformation is not an easy process.

It requires a commitment and a continuous dedication to explore our own inner being and overcome the limitations of our mind. However, the end result is worth the effort. Spiritual transformation allows us to experience life to its fullest and find a deeper sense of purpose and meaning in our lives.

In this book, I will guide you on your journey to spiritual transformation. I will provide you with tools and techniques to help you explore your own inner self and overcome the limitations of your mind.

I'll show you how you can find a deeper sense of purpose and meaning in your life and experience life to its fullest.

As we continue on this journey together, I encourage you to keep an open heart and mind. Spiritual transformation is not an easy process, but with commitment and dedication, you can experience a more fulfilling life.

Allow yourself to be guided by your own inner being and discover your true nature. Together, we can find enlightenment and transform our lives in positive and meaningful ways.

The power of beliefs

" How our limiting beliefs affect us "

Our beliefs are the driving force behind our actions and behaviors. Each of us has a set of beliefs that guide our decisions, and these beliefs are often formed during our childhood and youth.

If our beliefs are positive and move us forward, they can help us achieve our goals and objectives. However, if our beliefs are limiting, they impede our personal growth and development.

The programming we receive during our childhood can have a great impact in our adult life. Often, we absorb the beliefs and values of our parents and society without questioning them.

These programming can limit our ability to see the world differently and to find our own truth.

In the book "The Fifth Agreement", the authors suggest that it is important to question our programming and free ourselves from it in order to find our true personal freedom.

On the other hand, limiting beliefs are those that prevent us from achieving our goals and objectives. They often limit us through our way of thinking and perceiving the world around us.

Limiting beliefs can be the result of negative experiences in the past, negative messages we have received from others, or even our own insecurities and fears.

It is important to recognize our limiting beliefs in order to overcome them.

If we are not aware of these beliefs, they can continue to limit our personal growth and potential.

Recognizing our limiting beliefs is the first step towards positive change.

To identify our limiting beliefs, we must carefully examine our way of thinking and perceiving the world. We must ask ourselves if our beliefs are based on real facts or are simply our own interpretation of things.

We must ask ourselves if our beliefs propel us forward or hold us back.

Once we have identified our limiting beliefs, we must work on changing them. This can be a difficult process and requires commitment and dedication, but it is essential to our personal growth and success.

One way to change our limiting beliefs is through mental reprogramming. Mental reprogramming is a process in which we replace our limiting beliefs with positive and powerful beliefs.

This involves changing our way of thinking and perceiving the world, and it can help us overcome our fears and limitations.

Another way to overcome our limiting beliefs is through creative visualization. Creative visualization is a process in which we imagine ourselves reaching our goals and objectives. This helps us overcome our fears and limitations and allows us to focus on our strengths and abilities.

Meditation can also be a powerful tool to overcome our limiting beliefs. Meditation helps us calm down and focus on the present moment.

This allows us to overcome our fears and limitations and helps us find a deeper sense of peace and inner balance.

In short, our beliefs are the driving force behind our actions and behaviors. If our beliefs are limiting, they can impede our personal growth and success.

Identifying and overcoming our limiting beliefs is essential to our personal growth and success.

Through mental reprogramming, creative visualization, and meditation, we can overcome our limiting beliefs and reach our true potential.

Identify your thought patterns

"What is preventing you from moving forward?"

One of the keys to transforming our life is through changing habits.

Our habits are patterns of behavior that have become ingrained in our daily lives, and they are either positive or negative.

If we want to achieve our goals and objectives, it is essential that we have positive habits that propel us forward.

The first step to changing our habits is to identify the habits we want to change.

This may involve a close examination of our daily routine and the behavior patterns we follow.

We must ask ourselves if our habits are helping us reach our goals or if they are holding us back.

Once we have identified the habits we want to change, we must set clear and specific goals for the change.

It is important to keep in mind that changing habits does not happen overnight, and that it takes time and effort to reach our goals.

An effective way to change our habits is through substitution. This involves replacing a negative habit with a positive one.

For example, if we want to quit smoking, we could substitute the habit of exercising regularly.

Another effective way to change our habits is through the implementation of habits in small steps.

This involves making gradual changes to our behavior patterns, rather than trying to make drastic changes all at once.

For example, if we want to start exercising regularly, we might start by walking for 10 minutes a day and then gradually increase the time and intensity of the exercise.

It is also important to note that habits are related to our beliefs and thoughts. If we think we can't change a habit, we probably won't.

Therefore, it is essential to work on our negative beliefs and thoughts in order to change our habits effectively.

To maintain our new habits, it is important to establish a daily routine that includes time dedicated to changing habits.

This may involve planning specific activities and creating a detailed schedule to follow.

In short, changing our habits is an essential part of transforming our lives.

Identifying the habits we want to change, setting clear and specific goals, and using techniques such as substitution and implementing habits in small steps are keys to success.

It is also important to work on our negative beliefs and thoughts in order to change our habits effectively.

By establishing a daily routine dedicated to changing habits, we can maintain our new habits and achieve our goals and objectives.

Changing your habits

" Small actions that make a big difference "

Limiting beliefs are negative thoughts that we have accepted as true, and that prevent us from reaching our goals and objectives.

These limiting beliefs can be embedded in our subconscious mind, and can have a significant impact on our daily lives.

To transform our life, it is essential to work on our limiting beliefs. The first step is to identify the limiting beliefs that are holding us back.

This may involve an honest and detailed self-assessment of our thoughts and behaviors.

Once we have identified our limiting beliefs, we must question their veracity.

It is important to ask ourselves if these beliefs are really true or if we have simply accepted them as true.

Limiting beliefs are often the result of past experiences or negative comments from other people, and are not based on hard facts.

Once we have challenged our limiting beliefs, we must replace them with more positive and empowering beliefs.

This involves focusing on our strengths and capabilities, and recognizing that we are capable of achieving our goals and objectives.

Another effective way to work on our limiting beliefs is through visualization.

Visualization involves imagining positive scenarios and visualizing ourselves reaching our goals and objectives. This will help us change our mindset and overcome limiting beliefs that are holding us back.

It is also important to surround ourselves with positive and motivating people who support us in our transformation.These people can help us maintain a positive mindset and overcome our limiting beliefs.

In short, working on our limiting beliefs is essential to transform our lives.

Identifying and questioning our limiting beliefs, replacing them with more positive and empowering beliefs, and using techniques like visualization and surrounding ourselves with positive people are key to overcoming our limiting beliefs and reaching our goals and objectives.

By working on our limiting beliefs, we can unlock our potential and transform our lives for the better.

Here I provide you with 6 steps that you can follow to detect and modify negative habits in your day to day:

1.   Identify the negative habit: First, you must identify the negative habit you want to change. Ask yourself what behavior you want to change.

2. Analyze the underlying causes: Once you have identified the habit, analyze the underlying causes of the habit. What leads you to make that negative habit? What triggers it? How does it make you feel after doing it?

3. Find positive alternatives: Once you've identified the underlying causes of the habit, look for positive alternatives to replace it.

What positive habit can you adopt instead?

How does that positive habit make you feel?

4. Practice the new habit: Start practicing the new positive habit and make it a regular part of your day. It can be helpful to set goals and reminders to help you stay focused.

5. Be consistent: For the new habit to become an integral part of your day to day, you must be consistent. Be sure to incorporate it into your daily routine and stay focused on your goals.

6. Celebrate your achievements: every time you manage to change a negative habit for a positive one, celebrate your achievement. Take a moment to acknowledge your progress and to motivate yourself to continue to improve.

Creative Visualization

" How to use it to achieve your goals"

The power of habits in our lives is undeniable.

Habits can be both positive and negative and can have a significant impact on our physical, emotional, and mental health.

To transform our life, it is essential to work on our habits.

The first step to working on our habits is to identify the habits we want to change.

This may require an honest and detailed self-assessment of our current habits.

Once we have identified the habits we want to change, we need to focus on replacing them with more positive and healthy habits.

To change a negative habit, it is important to understand why we do it.

Negative habits are often the result of ingrained thought and behavior patterns in our subconscious mind. To change a habit, we must address the underlying causes of that habit and work on changing those thought and behavior patterns.

An effective way to change a negative habit is to set clear and achievable goals.

For example, if we want to quit smoking, we can set a goal to gradually reduce the number of cigarettes we smoke each day.

By setting clear and achievable goals, we can stay motivated and focused on our goal.

Another effective way to change a negative habit is through visualization.

Visualization involves imagining positive scenarios and visualizing ourselves practicing healthier habits.

This can help us change our mindset and overcome negative habits that are holding us back.

It is also important to establish a reward system to celebrate our achievements on the path to creating healthier habits.

The rewards can be small, like taking a relaxing bath after working out, or big, like a special dinner to celebrate a major milestone on our journey toward creating a new habit.

In summary, working on our habits is essential to transform our lives. Identifying the habits we want to change, understanding the underlying causes of those habits, setting clear and achievable goals, using visualization, and establishing a reward system are keys to overcoming negative habits and creating more positive and healthy habits.

By working on our habits, we can improve our physical, emotional, and mental health, and transform our lives for the better.

Here are 7 tips on how to set up an effective rewards system:

1. Be specific: Rewards should be specific and related to the habit you are trying to change. For example, if you're trying to exercise regularly, a good reward might be buying new workout clothes or signing up for a fitness class you've always wanted to try.

2. Make the rewards attractive: The rewards should be attractive enough to motivate you to keep going. If you're not excited about the reward, you're less likely to push yourself to reach your goal. Try to think of rewards that really excite and inspire you.

3. Set clear goals: Clear and achievable goals are essential to establishing an effective reward system. Make sure the goals you are setting are realistic and achievable, otherwise you will quickly become demotivated.

4. Celebrate small achievements: Don't wait until you've reached the end goal to celebrate your accomplishments. Celebrate every small step you take towards your goal. This will help you stay motivated and focused on your ultimate goal.

5. Vary your rewards: Changing the rewards from time to time can make the system more exciting and motivating. Try to think of different types of rewards, from small daily rewards to large rewards for reaching major milestones on your way to creating a new habit.

6. Be consistent: Consistency is key when it comes to establishing an effective reward system. Make sure that you are following your rewards plan regularly and that you are consistently celebrating your achievements.

7. Adjust your reward system as needed: If you find that your reward system isn't working, feel free to adjust it as needed. Try different types of rewards and adjust your goals and rewards based on your needs and preferences.

Remember that the goal of a reward system is to keep you motivated and focused on your goals. If you find that they are not working for you, do not give up. Keep experimenting and adjusting until you find a system that works for you.

Mindfulness

" Learn to be present at that precise moment and free yourself from your stress "

In the previous chapter, we talked about the importance of establishing an effective reward system to help you achieve your goals.

Stress is a natural part of life, but when it becomes constant, it can have a negative impact on mental and physical health. People can experience stress due to various reasons, such as pressure at work, interpersonal relationships, health, and financial problems.

The good news is that there is a meditation technique that can help people reduce stress and find inner peace: mindfulness.

Mindfulness practice involves being fully present in the present moment and focusing on your breath and bodily sensations without judging them.

By practicing mindfulness, you can train your mind not to worry about the past or the future, but simply to improve in the present moment.

Through regular practice, people can learn not to hold on to negative thoughts and emotions, but simply let them go and accept what is.

Mindfulness practice can also help reduce stress levels by decreasing emotional reactivity. Instead of automatically reacting to a stressful stimulus, you can take a moment to observe the thoughts and emotions that arise and respond in a more conscious and thoughtful way.

Additionally, mindfulness practice can help people improve their resilience to stress. Instead of feeling overwhelmed and discouraged by life's challenges, people can learn to face them with a more positive attitude and clearer mind.

For those looking to start their own mindfulness practice, there are many ways to go about it. People can start with a guided meditation online or attend a meditation group in person.

Mindfulness can also be practiced during daily activities, such as walking, eating, or even doing the dishes.

In conclusion, mindfulness practice is a valuable tool for those seeking to reduce stress and find inner peace.

By learning to be fully present in the present moment and accepting what is, people can improve their resilience to stress and improve their overall mental and physical health.

With regular practice, mindfulness can be a valuable tool for de-stressing and finding inner peace amid the chaos of modern life.

Here are 11 tips for practicing mindfulness effectively:

1.   Establish a schedule for daily mindfulness practice. You can start with five minutes a day and then gradually increase the time.

2.   Find a quiet place without distractions to practice mindfulness meditation.

3.   Breathing is essential in the practice of mindfulness. You can start with a simple technique, like counting your breaths.

4.   Accept your thoughts without judging them. Allow them to flow without holding on to them or trying to control them.

5.   Pay attention to your body. Be aware of the sensations in your body while you meditate.

6.   Guided meditation is a great way to start practicing mindfulness. There are many apps and videos online that offer guided meditations.

7.   Don't give up. Don't expect immediate results. Mindfulness practice takes time and effort.

8. Don't judge yourself if you get distracted or your mind wanders during meditation. It's normal and that happens to everyone at first.

9. Make it part of your daily routine: Incorporate the practice of mindfulness into your daily routine so that it becomes a habit.

10. Be patient: The practice of mindfulness requires patience and perseverance. Be patient with yourself as you develop this skill.

11. Practice gratitude: Practice gratitude during mindfulness meditation. Give thanks for the positive things in your life and for the opportunity to practice mindfulness.

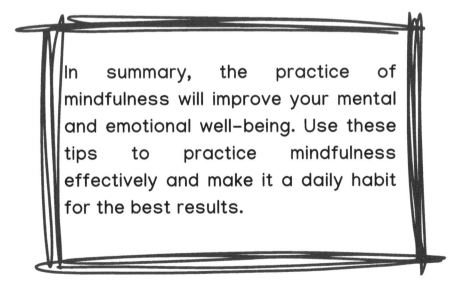

In summary, the practice of mindfulness will improve your mental and emotional well-being. Use these tips to practice mindfulness effectively and make it a daily habit for the best results.

The importance of self-esteem

" How to learn to love yourself "

Self-esteem is a central issue in personal growth and happiness in life.

The way we feel and think about ourselves affects all areas of our lives, including our relationships, work, health, and emotional well-being. Having a healthy self-esteem is essential to feeling fulfilled and happy in life.

Self-esteem is the evaluation we have of ourselves. It is based on the perception we have of our own capacity, abilities, values and achievements.

Healthy self-esteem allows us to feel self-assured and capable of facing life's challenges, while low self-esteem can make us feel insecure, helpless, and even worthless.

Developing a healthy self-esteem is not something that is achieved overnight, rather it is a process that takes time and effort.

10 ways we can work on our self-esteem

1.　　Identify your strengths: We all have abilities and positive qualities. Take the time to identify your strengths and abilities and learn to value and appreciate them.

2.　　Learn to accept your weaknesses: It is also important to recognize that we all have areas in which we need to improve. Learn to accept your weaknesses and work on them constructively.

3.　　Be kind to yourself: Try to be kind and compassionate to yourself. Instead of harshly criticizing or judging yourself, practice self-compassion and empathy.

4.　　Surround yourself with positive people: The people we spend time with can influence our self-esteem. Surround yourself with positive and supportive people who make you feel valued and loved.

5.　　Learn to say NO: Learn to set healthy boundaries and say no when necessary. Don't feel compelled to do things you don't want to do or don't feel good about yourself.

6.   Practice self-care: Self-care is fundamental to our self-esteem. Make sure you take care of your body, mind and spirit in a healthy and constructive way.

7.   Celebrate your achievements: Learn to celebrate your achievements, no matter how small. Recognize your achievements and learn to be proud of yourself.

8.   Learn to handle criticism: Criticism can be difficult to handle, but it is important to remember that it is not always personal. Learn to receive constructive criticism openly and to handle negative criticism in a healthy way.

9.   Do things that make you feel good: Spend time doing things that you enjoy and that make you feel good about yourself. This can include activities like exercise, meditation, reading, or just spending time with friends and family.

10.   Seek help if you need it: If you are struggling with your self-esteem, do not hesitate to seek help. Talk to a trusted friend, therapist, or life coach for support and guidance.

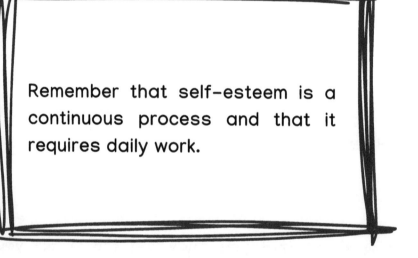

Remember that self-esteem is a continuous process and that it requires daily work.

Managing your emotions

" Tools to regulate your emotional states "

Emotions are a fundamental part of our lives and allow us to connect with the world around us. However, they can be overwhelming and even paralyzing at times, especially if we don't know how to handle them properly.

In this chapter, we will explore 6 useful tools to help you regulate your emotional states.

The first tool is self-awareness

To manage your emotions, it is important that you can recognize and name them. Many times, we feel overwhelmed by an emotion and we don't know exactly what we are feeling. Taking a moment to stop and pay attention to what's going on inside of you can go a long way in understanding your emotions.

Take a few minutes to breathe deeply and focus on your body.   How does your body feel?

Is there a place where you notice tension or discomfort?

What emotion are you experiencing?

How would you describe it?

The second tool is meditation

Meditation helps calm your mind and reduce the intensity of your emotions. There are many different ways to meditate, but one common practice is to focus on your breath. Find a quiet place and sit comfortably. Close your eyes and take a deep breath, concentrating on the sensation of the air moving in and out of your body. If your mind wanders, don't worry; just come back to your breath.

The third tool is physical exercise

Exercise is an effective way to release tension and reduce stress. Plus, it can improve your mood and help you feel more energetic and positive. Find an activity you enjoy, whether it's running, yoga, or walking in nature, and do it regularly.

The fourth tool is creativity

Creativity is a powerful way to express your emotions and release tension. Whether through writing, music, painting, or any other form of art, finding a creative outlet can help you process your emotions and give them a safe place to exist. It's not about being a professional artist, it's about exploring what makes you feel good and giving it space in your life.

The fifth tool is social support

Sometimes when we feel overwhelmed by our emotions, we need the help of other people to feel better. Find trusted people with whom you can talk about your emotions and who offer support and understanding. This can be a friend, family member, or therapist. Remember that asking for help is not a weakness, but a show of courage and authenticity.

The sixth tool is visualization

Visualization involves creating positive mental images to help you feel better. You can close your eyes and imagine yourself in a calm and safe place, surrounded by things that make you feel good. You can also visualize yourself successfully and calmly handling a difficult situation.

Emotions are a fundamental part of our experiences, and can significantly influence our decisions and actions. However, sometimes emotions can be overwhelming, which can lead to irrational and impulsive decision making. That is why it is important to learn to manage our emotions and regulate our emotional states.

11 more tools that will help you manage your emotions and regulate your emotional states:

1.   Before you can manage your emotions, you need to be able to identify them. Learn to recognize the different types of emotions and how they feel in your body. Identifying your emotions will help you have a clearer understanding of your feelings.

2.   Mindfulness is a practice that helps you be present in the moment and focus on the here and now. By practicing mindfulness, you learn to observe your emotions without judging them and without getting swept up in them.

3.   Our thoughts can amplify our negative emotions. For example, if you have a negative thought about yourself, it can make you feel sad or angry. Learn to change your negative thoughts to more positive and realistic thoughts.

4.   Talking to someone you trust helps you process your emotions and feel better. Find a friend, family member, or therapist with whom you can talk openly and without judgment.

5.   Exercise is a great way to release emotional tension and reduce stress. When you move, you release endorphins, which are feel-good chemicals.

6.   Lack of sleep makes you feel more irritable and emotionally sensitive. Make sure you get enough sleep so that you have the energy and mental clarity to face the day.

7.   Practice deep breathing: Deep breathing is a relaxation technique that helps you reduce stress and anxiety. By taking a deep breath, you fill your lungs with air and give your body a signal to relax.

8.   Learning to say "no" is the best way to protect your emotional boundaries. Learn to set healthy boundaries and say "no" to things that don't serve you.

9. Healthy relationships provide you with emotional support and help you feel safe and loved. Look for relationships that are mutually beneficial and where you both support each other emotionally.

10. Gratitude is an effective way to change your mood and improve your emotional well-being. Take the time to focus on the positive things in your life and be thankful for them.

11. If your emotions are significantly affecting your daily life and you cannot manage them on your own, seek professional help.

The Law of Attraction

" How to use it to attract what you want in your life "

The law of attraction is a concept that has gained a lot of popularity in the world of personal growth in recent years. The basic idea behind this law is that you can attract what you want into your life simply by focusing on it in a positive way and believing that it is possible.

In this chapter, we'll explore this idea further and provide practical tools to help you use the Law of Attraction in your daily life.

To begin with, it is important to understand that the law of attraction is not a magic or instant solution to all your problems.

You can't just sit and visualize something and expect it to appear in front of you. Instead, the law of attraction is a gradual and ongoing process that requires time, effort, and patience.

The first step to using the law of attraction effectively is to clearly define what you want.

This may seem obvious, but many people have a hard time articulating exactly what they want in life.

Take the time to reflect on what really matters to you and what you want to achieve. Once you've defined your goals, write them down and visualize them in vivid detail.

The next step is to cultivate a positive and optimistic attitude. The law of attraction is based on the belief that what you focus on expands, so if you focus on negative and limiting thoughts, that is what you will attract into your life.

Instead, focus on positive thoughts and visualize your goals as having already been achieved.

It is also important to trust yourself and your abilities. Doubt and fear block you, so make sure you believe in yourself and your possibilities.

Keep an open mind and welcome new opportunities and experiences, even if they seem different than what you had in mind.

Another important tool to use the law of attraction is gratitude. Practice gratitude daily by focusing on the positive things you already have in your life. Give thanks for the big and small things, and focus on the things that make you feel good and happy.

Gratitude increases your energy and positive vibration, which in turn will attract more positive things into your life.

Finally, it is important to take action and work towards your goals. The Law of Attraction is not a substitute for action, but rather works best in combination with it.

Take concrete steps to achieve your goals and maintain a positive mindset as you work towards them.

In summary, the law of attraction is a powerful tool to attract what you want into your life, but it requires constant effort and a positive attitude.

Define your goals clearly, cultivate a positive mindset, trust yourself and your abilities, practice gratitude, and take concrete action toward your goals.
With these tools, you can use the law of attraction to manifest a life filled with success, happiness, and personal fulfillment.

The Power of Language

" How changing the way you speak can change your life "

The language we use has a great impact on our lives. The way we talk about ourselves, others, and our situations can affect our self-esteem, our relationships, and our outlook on life. In this chapter, you will learn how changing the way you speak will change your life.

Speak positively about yourself. Talk about yourself with love and respect. Avoid criticizing yourself and focusing on your weaknesses. Instead, talk about your strengths and accomplishments. The way you talk to yourself is going to affect your self esteem and confidence.

Avoid negative language and words that make you feel bad about yourself. Words like "never", "always", "I can't" or "I'm a failure" have a negative impact on your life. Instead, focus on positive language and words that make you feel good about yourself.

Talk about your goals in positive terms.

Instead of saying "I don't want to be single," say "I want to be in a happy and healthy relationship."

Speaking in positive terms can help you focus on what you want instead of what you want to avoid.

Be aware, your body language is very imposing and affects how you perceive yourself and how others perceive you.

Maintain a confident posture and speak with confidence to feel more confident in yourself.

Use language to motivate yourself and achieve your goals.

Instead of saying "I can't do it," say "I'm going to try and do my best to make it."

Motivating language will help you stay motivated and overcome obstacles.

Talk about others in positive terms. Instead of focusing on the weaknesses of others, focus on their strengths and what makes them unique.

Positive affirmations are positive statements that you repeat to yourself to reinforce a positive belief.

For example, "I am worthy of love and respect" or "I have the skills and confidence to achieve my goals." Positive affirmations help you change your limiting thoughts and beliefs.

Humor is a powerful tool for changing your perspective and reducing stress. Use humor to see things from a different perspective and to not take everything so seriously.

Speak with intention and think before you speak. This allows you to be more aware of your language and how it can affect your life.

Practice, practice, practice: Changing the way you speak takes practice. Practice using positive and encouraging language every day.

Embracing uncertainty

" How to learn to live without fear of change "

In life, change is inevitable. We often resist uncertainty and prefer to stay in our comfort zone.

But what if we learned to embrace uncertainty and accept change as a natural part of life?

Uncertainty can be a source of stress and anxiety. We are concerned about the future and what may happen.

However, if we can change our perspective and see uncertainty as an opportunity to grow, we can begin to embrace it rather than fear it.

The first step to embracing uncertainty is accepting that change is inevitable.

Life is constantly evolving and we cannot control everything that happens around us. Sometimes things don't turn out the way we expect, but that doesn't mean we should fear the future.

Instead of focusing on fear and anxiety, we can learn to focus on what is within our control. We can work on improving our mindset and building resilience to face whatever challenges come our way.

Another important step in embracing uncertainty is cultivating self-confidence. When we are confident in our abilities and strengths, we feel more confident and capable of facing any change that comes our way.

We can build our confidence by setting realistic goals and working hard to achieve them.

It is also important to keep a positive attitude and be optimistic. Instead of focusing on the negative, we can learn to see challenges as opportunities to grow and improve.

By maintaining a positive attitude, we can feel more motivated and prepared to face any change that comes our way.

Another way to embrace uncertainty is to learn to adapt. When things don't go our way, we can learn to adapt to the situation and find new ways of doing things. We can be flexible and open to new ideas and perspectives.

It is also important to remember that we are not alone. We can seek support from friends and family, and we can also seek help from professionals like a therapist.

By having a support network, we can feel more confident and able to face any change that comes our way.

In short, embracing uncertainty means accepting that change is inevitable and learning to see it as an opportunity to grow. We can build our confidence, maintain a positive attitude, and learn to adapt to changing situations. By doing so, we can live without fear of change and be open to all the possibilities that life has to offer.

I am going to tell you the true story of Ana, this is not her real name but I am sure that when you read it you will know that it is you, with permission.

Ana who had always been very self-demanding and feared that she was not good enough at her job and in her life in general. She felt trapped in a life that did not make her happy and longed for a change.

After much reflection, Ana decided to quit her secure and stable job to start her own business. It was a leap of faith and it took her some time to adjust, but she finally found the success and happiness she had been searching for.

Ana once told me, "I realized that to achieve something you've never had, you must do something you've never done." This famous quote from Thomas Jefferson reflects very well the process that Ana went through when leaving her comfort zone and risking doing something new and different.

Over time, Ana felt more secure and confident in herself. She realized that the fear of failure had been holding her back, but in facing it, she had discovered new possibilities and achieved great personal growth.

Today, her business has grown and is very successful, and Ana feels happy and fulfilled in her work and in her life in general.

This story demonstrates how getting out of your comfort zone can be scary, but it can also be a source of growth and happiness.
By facing our fears and taking risks, we can discover our true potential and achieve incredible goals that we never imagined we could achieve.

The importance of action

" How to move from theory to practice "

Often, we find ourselves in the situation where we have a theoretical knowledge or an idea of what we want to achieve, but we don't know how to carry it out.

It's easy to get caught up in theory and planning, but without action, no real change will occur in our lives.

Action is the key component to transform our lives and achieve our goals.

However, it can be difficult to take the first step and put into practice what we have learned or planned.

In this chapter, we will explore the importance of action and how we can overcome the obstacles that prevent us from taking that first step.

The first step in moving from theory to practice is to understand why we are not acting.

Often, fear of failure, a lack of self-confidence, and a lack of clarity about what we want to achieve can prevent us from taking the first step.

To overcome these obstacles, we must start by building confidence in ourselves and our abilities. We can do this by taking small steps and gradually increasing the level of difficulty.

In addition, it is important to establish clear and specific goals to know what we want to achieve and how we are going to do it.

Goals need to be realistic and achievable, but they also need to be challenging enough to motivate us to take action.

Another way to overcome obstacles to taking action is to make an action plan.

This involves breaking down our goals into smaller, achievable steps, and setting realistic deadlines for each one.

The action plan helps us avoid feeling overwhelmed and focus on the individual steps we need to take to achieve our goals.

Also, it is important to remember that the action is not always perfect.

We can make mistakes, experience failure, and face challenges along the way.

The important thing is to learn from them and move on. In fact, failures can be a valuable opportunity to learn and grow, and can provide the motivation we need to keep going.

It is also important to stay motivated as we move towards our goals. One way to do this is to celebrate our accomplishments along the way, even the smallest ones.

Every step we take brings us a little closer to our ultimate goal, and acknowledging our accomplishments can help us stay motivated and focused.

In short, action is essential to transform our lives and achieve our goals. To overcome the obstacles that prevent us from taking the first step, we must build confidence in ourselves, set clear and specific goals make a plan of action and remember that failures are an opportunity to learn and grow.

Staying motivated and celebrating our achievements is also key to staying focused and moving towards our goals. With determination, patience, and action, we can transform our lives and achieve our most ambitious goals.

Overcoming the fear of failure

" Learn to see mistakes as opportunities
for growth "

Fear of failure is one of the biggest barriers that prevent people from reaching their goals and dreams.

The fear of not being good enough, of failing, or of not meeting expectations can paralyze us and make us stop trying.

However, failure is a natural part of the learning and growth process, and we must learn to see it as an opportunity to improve and advance.

First of all, it is important to remember that failure is not something personal. We should not associate our mistakes with our identity or worth as people.

Instead, we need to understand that mistakes are a natural part of the learning process, and that even the most experienced professionals make mistakes.

One of the keys to overcoming the fear of failure is to change our perception of it.

Instead of seeing it as a threat, we need to start seeing it as an opportunity to learn and grow.

Errors can help us identify our weaknesses and areas for improvement and can provide us with valuable information that allows us to adjust our approach and improve in the future.

Another important aspect of overcoming the fear of failure is learning to let go of perfectionism.

Many people are afraid of failure because they have high expectations of themselves and feel the pressure to be perfect.

However, perfection does not exist, and trying to achieve it can be exhausting and impossible to achieve.

Instead, we must accept that making mistakes is natural and we must not be so hard on ourselves when we do.

The growth mindset is another powerful tool to overcome the fear of failure.

Instead of seeing skills as fixed and unchangeable, we need to understand that we can improve and develop our skills with practice and effort.

We must see mistakes as an opportunity to learn and improve, rather than as a sign that we are not good enough.

Finally, it is important to have a positive attitude towards failure. Instead of feeling defeated or discouraged when we make a mistake, we should try to see it as an opportunity to grow and improve. We should celebrate our mistakes and learn from them, instead of feeling ashamed or defeated.

In conclusion, overcoming the fear of failure is a fundamental step to achieve our goals and dreams. We must change our perception of failure and see it as an opportunity to learn and grow, instead of a threat.

We must let go of perfectionism and have a growth mindset, and have a positive attitude towards failure. By doing so, we can free ourselves from fear and begin to reach our full potential.

Breathing into your inner calm

Conscious breathing is a very effective practice for improving physical, mental and emotional health.

As a therapist I have seen how this practice can transform people's lives and help them find greater inner peace.

In this chapter, I want to share with you some of the benefits of mindful breathing and how to start incorporating it into your daily life.

First of all, mindful breathing helps reduce stress and anxiety. When we are stressed or anxious, our breathing becomes rapid and shallow, which can make our symptoms worse.

Mindful breathing helps us reconnect with our natural breath and reduce tension in our body.

To practice mindful breathing, simply take a few minutes to sit in a quiet, comfortable place.

Close your eyes and bring your attention to your breath. Observe how the air enters and leaves your body without trying to change it.

If your mind wanders, simply bring your attention back to your breathing.

Another benefit of mindful breathing is that it can help you improve your concentration and focus. When we practice mindful breathing, we train our mind to operate in the present moment.

This can be very helpful if you have difficulty concentrating at work or on your daily tasks.

In addition, conscious breathing also helps improve your mood and emotional well-being. When we breathe consciously, we send signals to the brain to release endorphins, the feel-good hormones.

This makes us feel happier and more relaxed.

Another important aspect of conscious breathing is that it allows us to connect with our bodies and our emotions.
Often in our daily lives, we become disconnected from our bodies and our emotions, which can lead to a feeling of disconnection and imbalance.

Mindful breathing helps us reconnect with our inner experience and listen to our needs.

In summary, conscious breathing is a very powerful tool to improve our physical, mental and emotional health.

It can help us reduce stress, improve our concentration and focus, improve our mood, and connect with our bodies and emotions.

If you want to start incorporating mindful breathing into your daily life, I suggest starting with a few minutes a day and gradually increasing.

You can also try different breathing techniques, such as diaphragmatic breathing or square breathing.

Remember that the practice of conscious breathing requires patience and consistency.

Don't be discouraged if you have trouble concentrating at first or are easily distracted.

Over time, mindful breathing will become a valuable tool for your emotional well-being and overall quality of life.

I am going to share a meditation with you so that you can practice the square meditation with me.

Let's start by finding a quiet and comfortable place to sit, preferably in a position where you can keep your spine straight and your body relaxed.

You can close your eyes if you find it easier to focus and start paying attention to your breathing.

Begin by inhaling deeply through your nose, slowly counting to four as you fill your lungs with air.

Feel how your abdomen and chest expand.
Hold your breath for four seconds, and then slowly exhale through your nose for a count of four as you empty your lungs of air.

Keep your lungs empty for four seconds before inhaling again.

Continue breathing in this way for several cycles, feeling the connection to your breath and your body.

As you continue to breathe in this way, you can imagine that you are creating a square shape with your breath.

Each inhalation and exhalation represents one side of the shape, and the four seconds that you spend in each phase represent the angles of the shape.

Imagine that you are drawing this shape in the air with your breath, feeling the stability and calm that the square shape brings you.

With each breath cycle, feel more and more relaxed and calm. If your mind wanders with thoughts or concerns, simply acknowledge them and then let them go, returning your attention back to your breath.

Continue breathing in this way for as long as you like, perhaps 4 to 8 minutes.

When you feel the time is right, allow your breathing to return to its natural rhythm.

Take a moment to notice how you feel right now and what changes you have experienced in your body and mind.

Feel free to sit down for a moment before continuing with your day.

I hope you find this meditation helpful and relaxing. Square breathing is a powerful tool to help calm the mind and body during times of stress and anxiety.

Remember that regular meditation practice will help you develop a deeper connection with your body and mind, and will have lasting benefits for your overall well-being.

Gratitude

" How a single thank you changes your life "

Gratitude is one of the most powerful emotions we can experience.

It is the feeling of recognition and appreciation for what we have and what surrounds us.

The act of being grateful not only has emotional benefits, but also has a positive impact on our physical and mental health.

When we practice gratitude, we focus on what we have instead of what we lack. This helps us to change our perspective and see life in a more positive way.

Instead of worrying about what we don't have, we focus on the blessings we already have in our lives.

Gratitude also helps us better manage stress and anxiety.

When we feel overwhelmed by life, we can take a moment to reflect on the things we are grateful for.

This can help us feel calmer and more at peace.

Also, gratitude improves our personal relationships.

When we are grateful for the people in our lives, we let them know that they are important to us.

This strengthens our emotional connections and makes us feel more connected to the people around us.

So how can we practice gratitude in our daily lives?

One way is to start a gratitude journal.

Every night before you go to bed, write down 3 things you are grateful for in your life.

It can be simple things like the sun shining in the sky or a moment of laughter with a friend.

By doing this, you train your mind to focus on the positive and cultivate gratitude as a regular part of your life.

Another way to practice gratitude is to express it to others.

You can send a text or a thank you note to someone who has been kind to you or made a positive impact in your life.

By doing so, you not only make the other person feel good, but it also makes you feel good.

Gratitude can also be practiced through meditation. Take a few minutes each day to meditate on the things you are grateful for.

Visualize these things in your mind and feel the feeling of gratitude in your body.

By doing so, you are strengthening positive emotions and reducing negative emotions.

In short, gratitude is a powerful emotion that can change our lives for the better.

By cultivating gratitude in our daily lives, we can change our perspective, improve our physical and mental health, strengthen our relationships, and live happier, more fulfilling lives.

Start practicing gratitude today and see how this Thank you transforms your life.

Conclusions and final advice

" How to continue transforming your life "

We have reached the end of this book and it is important to recap what we have learned throughout these pages.

We have talked about the importance of changing our limiting habits and beliefs in order to effectively transform our lives.

We have explored powerful tools such as meditation, mindfulness, visualization, and the law of attraction, among others, that allow us to work on ourselves and achieve our goals.

However, it is important to keep in mind that personal transformation is an ongoing process, and not a final destination.

There will always be new challenges and obstacles along the way, and it is our responsibility to learn how to deal with them effectively.

Next, I remind you of the most important tips so that you can continue transforming your life:

1.   Maintain a positive attitude: The attitude you have towards life will greatly influence your ability to transform it. Maintain a positive mindset and focus on personal growth.

2.   Be grateful: Gratitude is a powerful tool that helps us maintain a positive outlook on life. Take time each day to reflect on the things you are grateful for. Say Thank You More Often.

3. Surround yourself with positive people: The environment in which you find yourself can influence your attitude and your habits. Try to surround yourself with people who support you on your path of personal transformation.

4.   Learn from your mistakes: Mistakes are part of the learning process. Instead of feeling sorry for them, learn from your mistakes and use them as an opportunity to grow.

5. Keep your long-term goals in mind and focus your actions on achieving them. Remember that personal transformation is an ongoing process, and that each action you take brings you one step closer to your goals.

6. Personal transformation does not happen overnight. Be patient with yourself and celebrate every little accomplishment you make.

7. Take time each day to do something that you enjoy and that makes you feel good about yourself. This will help you maintain a positive attitude and focus on your personal growth.

8. Don't be afraid to seek support when you need it. Talk to friends, family, or a therapist if you feel like you need help overcoming an obstacle.

9. Continue to explore new tools and techniques for personal growth. Be open to experiment and learn new things.

10. Celebrate every achievement you make on your path of personal transformation. Acknowledge the hard work you've put in and give yourself the credit you deserve.

After reading this book, I hope you have gained new tools and knowledge to transform your life.

There is no magic formula for success in personal growth, but there are certain principles and practices that you can apply to improve your emotional, mental, and spiritual well-being.

One of the keys to success in personal transformation is consistency.

It is important to be persevering and patient, since significant changes do not happen overnight.

It is a gradual process and requires dedication and continuous effort.

Self-awareness and self-knowledge are fundamental to personal growth. Take time to reflect on your thoughts, emotions, beliefs, and behaviors.

Identify your strengths and weaknesses, and work on them to improve. Don't be afraid to ask for help if you need it. Life is a shared path and it is important to support each other.

Remember the importance of self-care. Take time for yourself to rest, relax, and do activities you enjoy.

Take care of your body, your mind and your spirit, since they are all connected.

Focusing on the present and practicing mindfulness are also important for personal transformation.

The present is the only moment we really have, so learn to be present and enjoy each moment.

Practicing mindfulness helps you to be present in the moment and cultivate mindfulness in your daily life.

Finally, remember the importance of gratitude and joy in life.

Learn to appreciate what you have and find joy in the little things.

Life is full of ups and downs, but focusing on the positive can help us get through the tough times.

In summary, personal transformation is a continuous process and requires effort and dedication. I hope this book has provided you with some useful tools to help you in this process. Always remember to be kind to yourself and be patient.

I wish you all the best on your path Transform Your Life!

Susurros de Chamán

On the cover of my book, I have used feathers to symbolize the transformation and personal growth that we undergo throughout our spiritual evolution.

An intimate evolution that changes you from within to help you advance on your path towards your freedom, that which few reaches, but that from one moment to the next leads you towards the spirit.

For me, the spirit is the soul of everything that surrounds us, that which awakens our gifts and sensibilities, that which makes us different and unique.

Vibrate, Feel, and Be Happy.

Transform your life, pen by pen,
teaching to teach...

Before I say goodbye and leave you my details, I want to thank you for choosing my book as you move towards awakening your own truth.

The path that some of us travel at some point in our lives to discover the true nature, the one that is hidden inside you. . I hope that my book has made your path easier.

For years, I have been posting periodically on my Facebook page the chamán Urbano.

https://www.facebook.com/Ichamanurbano

If you want to request information, you can send me a Whatsapp +34641314534

Milton Keynes UK
Ingram Content Group UK Ltd.
UKHW011104201123
432908UK00007B/1351